Sealed with love...

SEALED WITH LOVE

VOLUME 1

SWARNIKA

ISBN 979-888606712-5

Contents

Acknowledgements

This collection has been shaped beautifully with the contributions of Gauri Shukla, Nishtha Trehan, and Putul Mangni Mandal (Pooja Rai). I can't thank them enough for these gems adorning this collection.

Sealed With Love is written with love and presented to the readers with love. I thank the reader as well who reads these verses and dives into this pool of emotions along with us. Lastly, I would like to thank Notionpress for providing a platform for this book to be published.

Prologue

- *Swarnika*

Inking feelings baring my soul,
I write verse today.
Being vulnerable and at your mercy,
I write verse today.
Holding on to you
In this realm of fantasy
As you slip through me
In the real world,
I write verse today.
Forbidden for you to read
Yet written for you,
I write verse today.
Loving you once more,
I write verse today.
Finding my true self,
Even at the cost of
Losing you forever,
I write verse today.
Letting go finally,
I write verse today...

Featured Poets

Swarnika

Gauri Shukla

Nishtha Trehan

Putul Mangni Mandal

Swarnika

Swarnika is an avid reader and an ambivert. She is a glass-half-full kind of a person, not because she is always an optimist but because she believes that a glass that is full has no more scope and ends up creating the most amount of spills.

She completed her Bachelor's and Master's degree from the University of Delhi. She has completed her three-level professional certification in Spanish from Valencia Polytechnic University, Spain. She has also completed her certificate program in French from St. Stephen's College, University of Delhi. She is currently pursuing a Post-Graduate Diploma in Business Administration from Symbiosis Centre for Distance Learning, Pune. She is working on her thesis and research papers to earn her Ph.D. degree in English Literature. She has a keen interest in criminology and detective fiction. Writings that indulge mystery and rationale speak volumes to her. She has earned her TEFL and TESOL certificates as an English language teacher. She is also a certified dance teacher with specializations in Bharatnatyam, Kathak, and Contemporary. She is also certified in Classical Music and Fine Arts.

She believes in living in the moment rather than giving the moment the opportunity to live through you without you even realizing it. She has started her company- Nrityangana Kala Kendra OPC Private Limited on her own. She has been tutoring kids along with mentoring graduate and postgraduate students in academic and creative writing. On some days she is a dreamer while on others she is a realist. She firmly believes in humanism. Nature mesmerizes her.

She has initiated this project and has edited the book along with compiling it.

1. Long Time, No See...

- Swarnika

It has been a long time...
Long time as no pair of eyes wanted to see
Words were stained with blood
Bruises argued again
The strike of clock at twelve marked another end.

.

.

.

Mind wonders if love was a crime
Since none felt their souls were free
Complete silence today, tomorrow's emotional flood
That chapter ended and a new began
One finally moved on while the other continued to pretend.

2. What Love Was...

- Swarnika

She asked me what love was
And I did not know what to say.
I tried to figure out the perfect answer
But couldn't do it by the next day.

.

Failed in my conquest
I told her that I didn't have the perfect reply.
To which she said - perhaps you're right;
Love isn't sly.

.

You see, there is no perfect answer
To what love is or was.
Every vision presumes it differently
Gliding off the cause.

.

There is no perfect reply
As imperfect is this love.
Full of flaws and quirks
And yet it rises above.

3. What Love Isn't...

- Swarnika

The love that meets the eye
Isn't love at all.
Love doesn't change in a second
Unlike how one changes their look.

.

It isn't blind either
As none actually fall.
Love isn't a conquest
That you win by hook or by crook.

.

Love isn't losing track of time
Talking to someone over a call.
Love isn't picturesque
Like seen in movies or read in a book.

.

Perhaps love is not love
The love we percepted.
The ideals are apotheosized;
The real thing now hardly accepted.

.

Cherishing the idea to be in love
Real love dies a slow death.
Amidst the ideas, constraints, standards, and expectations
The real deal takes its last breath.

4. What Love Is...

- Swarnika

What is love?
Love is "what".
Just another question...
Asked by many
But truly known by none.
.
.
If you think love is that first glance-
Strangers across the room
Having conversations through their eyes;
'Love at first sight'
Repetitive glances and smiles,
Then you mistook love
For a vile of attraction.
But the vile isn't enough;
It'll perish.
Just like sleepless nights
Tossing and turning
Thinking about them;
Someone ruling the mind

Cannot reach heart.
Alveolus shrunk at the sight of
Obsession in disguise.

.

.

If you think love is
Falling for a good heart -
'Kindness is happiness';
'Soul is plenty'
Their aspirations shine,
Their achievements gloat,
Making you wonder to be
More like them than you.
Then again you're mistaken
With the glasses of admiration
Having a metallic rim of inspiration
And polished with idolization.

.

.

If the prospect of future
Makes the decisions for you
If you have to make
A list of pros and cons
If the perquisites have
Become essentials
If the balance of the relationship
Is similar to the bank balance

If you get excited in their company
Things seem interesting
Love is far away, my friend
And your interest will
Soon be killed.

.

.

Love for the sake of love -
Love because of the want to be loved.
Love because of being loved,
Love that gives,
Love that returns,
Love that reciprocates,
Isn't love...
Empathy has clouded your judgement.
You don't want to be left alone
In a room filled with people
But that doesn't mean
To love without the essence of love.

.

.

If love is what is written in books
Or what the camera captures,
If love is walking hand in hand
Sunsets and moony nights are serene,
If you can't keep your eyes off
Frisking hands, unwrapping legs,

If love is this to you -
You're mistaken again
But it isn't your fault
As you get consumed by desire.

.

.

If love makes you wonder,
If love makes you question,
If there is no absolute reason,
If ideals do not match,
If you're there without being there,
If they're here without being here,
If you're theirs
Not in person or soul,
Each is free -
A person of their own.
Apart yet together;
Different yet complimentary.
And if happiness is genuine,
If love confuses you
But still makes you smile,
If love makes you wonder
All the 'what's and 'why's,
Then you've found love
Or love has found you.
Don't let it pervade,
Don't let it evade;

Or else,

Love will allude you.

5. Lost and Found

– Swarnika

Nights wept,
The heart was broken.
None slept,
For granted they were taken.
Promises unkept,
They'd lost their token.
Paths intercept,
Souls were shaken.

.

.

Another pair of eyes
Wept that night,
Helplessly trying to help
Their little one;
For their love was real
They couldn't give up on.
Caressing the head
Of their little one to sleep,
The parent really woke up.

6. In Conundrum

– ***Swarnika***

This can't be sane;
All of it inane.
The plea of heart
To be a boon or bane;
The plea to heart
Could become inhumane.

.

Perhaps this is mundane
Or maybe it is profane;
The chaos in mind and
That of heart being germane.
Perhaps this will end up in a union
Or maybe breaking ane.

.

It'll crash or land like a plane,
Entangled in love's mane.
Faith in happily ever after
Or the fate of plain Jane;
Made of rock or broken by it
Either way the destined is stane.

7. Moving On

- Swarnika

I closed my eyes,
It was time for bed.
Something was missing
And something remained -
Some things unheard,
Some words unsaid.

.

I caught a flight
To a destination where
I was destined to be;
I was caught flying
Content lying bare.

.

Walking outside,
I see a face -
Familiar, kind, confused.
I wasn't recognized
Insignificant among humankind.
It was clear as water
And I was done with the chase.

.

I took a different gateway...
This time the travel
Won't be designed by fate
But I will hold the guns.
Firing up the sky
Fueled by strength,
I soar as I chose me
Self is what I unravel.

.

The destination isn't for
I'm on my way
And the eyes are open now
Siesta broken,
Yet I healed.
Finally, I could leave it all behind;
Things were limpid.
What I lost is insignificant now.
I found me,
That is all I have t say.

8. Our Book

*- **Swarnika***

Fingers sliding between
The edges of pages,
The crisp sheet
Creased at certain places
Enclosed with the weight
Of a hardcover
Hides truth
In the guise of tales
Allowing the forbidden,
Exposing the hidden;
Starts with the word
And ends with it
Painting a beautiful canvas
Of the unseen scenes.
Let it tell our story -
Lived by us,
Fantasized by the reader.
Let us recreate our world
And let the reader
Live it too

Through our eyes
No vices, no virtues
But our truth.
To the reader
It might be another story,
Tossing the book aside
Our book...
And moving on to another
Living it anew.
You and I will perish
But we will live on,
We will love
On the cover
Hushing at the rim.
These lines
Line up our story -
Words are days
And letters - hours;
Plain truth,
No embellishes,
Picked by another dreamer
Living our story.
Our book stays,
Our book remains,
Our book lives,
Our story breathes;
As you and I

are laid in the ground.

Gauri Shukla

Gauri Shukla is a third-year Literature student pursuing her passion for reading and writing from the University of Delhi. President of the Literary Society of the college, she is an avid reader who yearns to get lost in estranged, galvanic worlds of art. A national-level debater, she is someone who doesn't shy away from speaking her mind. An ardent scripturient, she has written articles for The Times of India, The Hindu, The Redstockings Chronicles, etc. She's currently working on a South-Asian anthology as an editor alongside editors from Bangladesh and Pakistan. Her lifelong dream is to document the experiences and sentiments of different people, belonging to different cultures, all around the world. She believes life is too short and time is fleeting thus, each moment needs to be savoured and felt to its optimum level. She likes to describe herself as a wandering cloud that romances with the sky, lost yet free.

9. What is love?

– Gauri Shukla

What is love if not the warmth of your body as it embraces mine?
What is love if not the smile that reaches your eyes every time you stop before a bookstore?
What is love if not the scent you give off after we've made love?
What is love if not the softness of your hands settled in mine?
What is love if not the sparkle in your eyes when you get mischievous?
What is love if not the handwritten letters that are smudged in places and written with so much thought?
What is love if not the coffee you place on my study table every evening?
What is love if not the soft snoring sounds you create that make me fall asleep at ease?
What is love if not the anxiety in your face when I fail to answer a call?
What is love if not the fierceness in the way you kiss me as tears of relief smear your beautiful face?
I am tainted with your love.

And unlike the ancient stars that burn and dissipate
Into radioactive remnants,
My heart shall burn for you eternally.
Because darling, you have me caught in an infinite loop of love.

10. Dozakh

- *Gauri Shukla*

(Dozakh means "a place of torment one believes they are in when separated from their lover"; hell)

.

I lose hope every day.
I know you exist.
Walking somewhere on this globe
In this ever-expanding menace of a world filled with too many shadows,
I know you exist.
I know you lust after eras long gone and seek joy in simple things.
I know you like sunsets more than sunrises and wouldn't miss the musky orange in the sky for anything.
I know you feel estranged in a place you feel like you don't belong to.
And I know you're looking for me as desperately as I am.
Running after vanishing dreams and invisible headlights
Crashing into speeding cars and getting into fights.
I feel tired and I lose a little hope every day.

I fear I'll lose the penumbra of your shadow I have entwined in my hands
If you stayed away any longer.
So, if you're as desperate as I am, look harder for me
So that, I can be purged from this hell
And spend the rest of my days buried in your arms.

11. A Dalliance

- Gauri Shukla

Small little glimpses of your face as you turn to look at something
The lip balm turning your glossy lips into a light pink shade
Your existence is a paradox, a contradiction that I could spend centuries studying
Without a thought to understanding; for you, I've even prayed.
I do not believe in God, just like I do not believe in love.
To me, love is like God; unattainable and invisible
Eternity and oblivion that leaves you writhing in pain all above
Devastated and burning in a new hell; of all things incapable.
I have memorized the slant of your brow and the wave in your hair,
The mole on your wrist and the rhythm of your steps.
The sunlight dancing on your face makes this world beautiful and fair
I am caught in a trance as you weave around me innumerable webs.
You haunt my thoughts with your marigold smile

You terrify me; unknown emotions swirling deep in the pit of my stomach
Call it the heart of a juvenile
But in you, I have found my muse; the perfect artwork.
You have the power to destroy me
And you don't even know it, you see?
I'm less afraid of dying than I am of losing you
And that scares me too.
I'm scared of you and of myself
Standing on a precipice is how it feels
I love you; I'll never say it out aloud
Even a little dalliance with you will be enough to last a lifetime for me.

Nishtha Trehan

Nishtha Trehan is a student at Atma Ram Sanatan Dharma College, University of Delhi, studying English Honours. In her breaks, she likes to read, write, and journal. It is under the guidance of her supervisor, Swarnika Singh, that she has been able to finish these poems.

12. Demons on her Mind

- Nishtha Trehan

Her demons start murmuring
Her inner conflicts enrage
Shredding her soul to pieces
Demons and angels alike.

.

Then the crowd turns to look at her
The gazes shoot like daggers
She wishes to escape, so does her demons
But not before her ignominy.

.

What's at fault is not the people
It's the demons that reside inside of her
The fiends, the parasites, the louts
They're always prying.

.

In the midst of her inner battle,
A pair of eyes lock onto hers
Gentle, they soften for her,
The demons quieten.

.

As the angel storms forward
No misdemeanor, he shakes his hands
Catching her eyes and promises to hold on for eternity
But an interminable existence is not enough.

.

For they take their vows
Owe to love each other forever and beyond
Now it's just him, her, and the dead demons
Is it really murder if the wife won't testify against her husband?

13. His Queen

- Nishtha Trehan

The photograph hangs on the wall,
Hands locked, eyes squinted in a smile,
The picture may have blurred
But the love has only strengthened.
My grandparents sit beneath it,
"Rani," a teasing whisper
Against my ears as I glance ahead
Mistaking the endearment for myself
An error of judgement, t'was
For our smiles mirror each other's
As my grandmother blushes
The only queen to exist in this household.

14. Shell of Marriage

- Nishtha Trehan

She works against the doctor's advice
Neglecting her bed rest
Her forehead creases in distress
As she complains of her poor health.

.

No one chooses to hear
Lips parted, eyes diverted, mouths shut
Her eyes cloud in regret
Cursing, whimpering, relenting.

.

This is her life, after all
A life without an embrace
So easily can she be replaced
She grieves.

.

Mourns the woman she could have been
Bemoans the woman she everyday kills
Sobs at the shell she now is
And wonders, if any of it was ever love.

Putul Mangni Mandal

Living in New Delhi, Putul Mangni Mandal was born in December 1996. It is a pseudonym that she has adopted for the literary world. By root, her family comes from Bihar and as mentioned in the name, she belongs to the Mandal community. However, she abhors rigid statism or communism. Putul (meaning doll; it is her mother's pet name) lives with her small family of four. Financially, she is lower middle class. She studied in a government school named Sarvodaya Co. Ed. Senior Secondary in Nanak Pura. She has done her Post Graduation in English from Delhi University and aspires to become a professional writer, too, among many other possible-impossible things.

Poems have fascinated her ever since she read Kanyadan, a poem by the famous romantic Hindi writer Suryakant Tripathi 'Nirālā' in tenth grade. But she never knew that she could write until the day when her teacher Minakshi Mehta asked the whole class to create something. She composed her first poem Lakshya. Since then, she has written many poems. Some of her English poems include On a Bus, Chores, Substitute, My Days, At Last, A Signal, and many others. She also writes in Hindi/Urdu and some of them are Intezar, Upar-Neechey, Bheetar, Chal, etc.

Fingers crossed, she hopes to soon come up with her poem collection. Not limiting herself to poems only, she has initiated in the field of prose writing through her first work Listen Didi which is a novella. Apart from this she also likes to write articles and essays on various literary topics. She hopes that people will find something interesting and unique in her work. If they do so, they may use her email address given below to express their useful views.

The three poems typed below are composed by Pooja Rai(Putul Mangni Mandal). The poems are based upon the theme of love. The first poem 'Acknowledgements' expresses the unacknowledged love which has been already perceived so by the guy she is in love with while The other poem 'Which Must be the Way?' on the contrary, is about a break up and the labour involved in its long process. Third and the last poem 'Your Loyal Pen' delineates a process of falling in love which should be a cycle that means it must not end with one break up.

15. Acknowledgements

*- **Putul Mangni Mandal***

Streaming in perennial cycles
The potential vows I often pledge,
I flush out when he's not around
But has never been acknowledged.

.

The frustrated tears of patience
Neither to him, I'm acknowledging
That often, I hide behind my eyes
When he asks how I am doing.

.

I claim my right on his every hour
Alas! nowhere but only in dreams
And how follows him my spy eyes
I will never acknowledge it to him.

.

The red hint that glows my cheeks
Finding his concerned hands warm
How will I be able to acknowledge
Placed gently on my unaware arm?

.

He splatters the acidic drops of oblivion
So, why should I ever acknowledge him?
The strange fever I've mysteriously caught
And why before him, my legs are limp?

.

Why I weave poetries in his memory
With the bleeding ink of my heart?
I have never acknowledged it to him
That he owns every number of my watch.

.

But naive this little heart of mine
Couldn't grasp a hint of the knowledge
That not even the slightest breath I own
He knows I don't need to acknowledge.

16. Which Must be the Way?

- Putul Mangni Mandal

In which way should I explain to you
The consequence of the cause
Behind not meeting you again?

.

Your falling eyes raise questions
They're repeated countless times
That my answers are wearing out
In the impetus of your unfailing tears
You pray must they flush away
And they, my solid upright answers
must never be found.

.

In search for new answers I admit,
I often find your cemented steps and
Your lonely wants that are whimpering
And hoping that our last meeting lasts forever.
In which way should I explain to you
The definition of the word 'last'?

.

Your love stares at me anxiously.
It tries to dig a hole in my memory
Perhaps to break in once again?
But I stomp them under my progressing steps
And push them below the unconscious soil.
Cautiously I leave no evidence of its presence.

.

For I've now let my mistakes past
For good.

17. Your Loyal Pen

- ***Putul Mangni Mandal***

A pen in hand brings
The levity of heart
And the obeying strings
Of passionate couplets
Irresistibly start…

.

Starts in the poetry
The unabated tales of love
Which shoots to eyes
A reckless intense rocket
That cracks above...

.

Cracks open the pain
Of the in-between distance
And hopes love for love
In exchange,
It takes a chance.

.

Chance that involves
Holding hand in hand

And to live every moment
As would one live
On a dreamland.

.

Dreams if the significant other
The ditto or the same if feels,
What else could one
Possibly want or would
Like to appeal.

.

But if the expectations somehow
Don't reach the goal
And the injury of love
On your body
Takes control,

.

Control your grief and come
Back to your pen
And to fill vacant pages again
Must you write
Another love poetry then.

9 798886 067125

Printed by Libri Plureos GmbH in Hamburg,
Germany